Cubs

by Norbert Landa

● A N I M A L   B A B I E S   S E R I E S ●

Cubs

English language version published by
Barron's Educational Series, Inc., 2000

Original title of the book in Spanish:
Ciencias y Manualidades de Animales Bebe

© Copyright Useful Books S.L., 2000
Barcelona, Spain (World Rights)

All inquiries should be addressed to:
Barron's Educational Series, Inc.
250 Wireless Boulevard
Hauppauge, New York 11788
http://www.barronseduc.com

Author of the scientific text: Norbert Landa
Author of the crafts text: Ona Pons
Crafts execution: Victoria Seix

Series graphic design: Estudi Guasch

Photography: Index and Age Fotostock
                    Nos & Soto

ISBN: 0-7641-1480-8

Library of Congress Catalog Card No. 99-068581

Printed in Spain
9 8 7 6 5 4 3 2 1

Cubs

Facts:

Fun:

How is your teddy bear today?

Touch his nose. If it is dry and warm, Teddy feels good. If it is cold and wet, you'd better put Teddy in bed!

Whether teddies are under the weather or feel fine, they always enjoy being with their best friend—you.

So when you look at the pictures in this book, make sure your teddy is at your side. He (or she) will love learning about real bears!

Are there bears in the woods ?

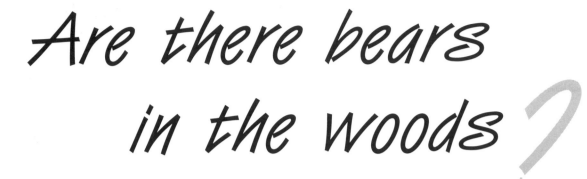

Well, that depends on where you live.

If you live in the cold polar regions, there are no woods outside, just ice fields and frozen sea. This is where polar bears live.

Do you live in the Australian bush? Then you might see a koala bear sleeping in a huge tree.

Where do you find pandas?

You might be lucky enough to encounter a panda, if you live in a Chinese bamboo jungle! However, there are very few pandas in the world, and they are very shy.

Or do you live far from any city, out in the wilderness, among mighty trees, wild streams, and huge waterfalls? These are places where black and brown bears live.

Most bears prefer living in the wilderness and far away from people.

Cubs

Do cubs need their mothers?

Just like your teddy bear needs you, cubs need their mothers
to take care of them.

Bears are mammals, just like dogs, cats, and cows.
This means they need to drink their mother's milk when they are small.

Cubs like milk very much, and they need it to become big and strong.

Cubs

Why don't cubs go to school ?

They have their mothers as teachers. They learn by being with her and imitating what she does. By doing the same things and eating the same foods, a cub finds out how to tell good mushrooms from bad ones.

He also learns how to find honey, when to eat berries, and how to catch a fish.

Cubs have to learn many skills because when they grow up, there will be no one to feed or take care of them anymore.

Do you take care of your teddy bear and teach him new things?

Do bears like honey?

Yes, they do. Most bears eat all kinds of food, but they prefer things that are sweet. And the sweetest thing they can usually find is honey from bees' nests that hang from trees. Fortunately, bears have thick fur and they do not mind being stung.

Bears also like berries, mushrooms, and even fresh grass. They also catch small animals, such as mice and rabbits. And, bears are very good at catching fish.

In fall, they have to eat a great deal to prepare for winter. When the cold weather comes, many kinds of bears go into a very long sleep. This is called hibernating, and they sleep in caves until spring comes.

What do polar bears, koala bears, and pandas eat ?

Polar bears are hunters. They are big, but they can run and swim very quickly. They hunt seals or catch fish and other sea animals for food.

Wild pandas mostly eat bamboo leaves because there is not much else to eat where they live. But pandas that live in the zoo also enjoy a good bowl of oats.

Koala bears only feed from the leaves of a tree called eucalyptus. They never seem to want anything different. They would rather starve!

Where do bears live ?

Bears are wild animals, and they are perfectly able to live out in the wilderness.

It is where they feel best. They need open space to roam and look for food. Unlike cats and dogs, bears are not animals you can keep as pets.

Bears can live happily in a zoo if proper care and ample space is provided. If you go to the zoo to see the bears, bring your teddy bear with you!

Cubs

You will need the following materials:

Color crayons (brown, yellow, orange, and black), a paper plate, red tissue paper, a pencil sharpener, and a stick of glue.

Create a cute cub to keep close to you.

My favorite picture

1 Draw the bear's eyes, nose, mouth, and ears in the center of the plate.

2 Sharpen the brown, yellow, and orange crayons over a dish. Do the same with the black crayon over another dish.

3 Spread glue all over the bear's face. Sprinkle some black crayon shavings over the bear's eyes, nose, and the line that marks the mouth. Distribute the color crayon shavings all over the rest of the bear's face. Let it dry.

Cubs

4 Tear the red tissue paper into small pieces and glue them around the face. They should cover the rest of the plate.

5 To hang your picture on the wall, you can use some double-face adhesive tape or a small adhesive hook.

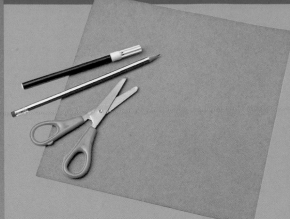

The three cubs learn by imitating their mother.

A family of brown bears

1 Cut out a square from the brown bristol and fold it in half.

2 Using the pattern you will find in the back of this book, draw a bear, aligning the back of the animal with the crease of the square folded in half.

3 Hold the folded bristol firmly together and cut out the bear outline with your scissors.

4 Fold the head down just from behind the ears.

5 Use the black marker to draw the bear's eyes, nose, mouth, and ears.

6 You can make big bears or small bears using the patterns in the back of this book.

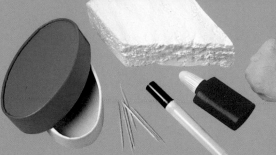

Brrrr! It's so cold in the polar regions!

Polar bears

1 Make a big clay ball to model the body, a small ball for the head, a long thin roll for the arms, and a thicker one for the legs. Cut both rolls in half lengthwise.

2 Stick a toothpick in each of the clay parts and attach it with some white glue. Now stick every clay part in place to form the whole body. Flatten out two small balls of clay to make the ears.

3 Line the outside of the small box with modeling clay, applying it with your fingers until the whole box is covered. Let it dry.

4 With the black marker, draw the bear's eyes, nose, mouth, and paws.

5 Glue the bears you have made to the top of the box. Put some styrofoam chunks behind them to look like big blocks of ice.

You will need the following materials:

White and black fabric, bristol board, scissors, a pencil, a black pen, white glue, and double-faced adhesive tape.

It is happy among bamboo canes.

The panda puppet

1 Draw all the puppet parts on the bristol board and use your scissors to cut them out. You will find the parts on page 30.

3 Place the template for the rest of panda parts over the black fabric and cut them out. Attach them to the cloth with some double-faced adhesive tape. Cut two ears and two spots for the eyes.

2 Place the template for the body over the white fabric, trace it twice and cut them out. Also cut out two small circles for the eyes.

4 Glue the ears to the top of one of the parts used for the body. Put glue all around the figure, but not on the bottom. Then, press the two parts that form the body together.

5 Now use some glue to attach arms, feet, eyes, a nose, and a mouth. Place something heavy on top of your panda until the glue dries.

6 You can have a puppet show with your finger puppet and pretend your panda is eating bamboo leaves.

You will need the following materials:

Corrugated cardboard (brown, pink, blue, and green), yellow and pink satin ribbons, small and large balloons (pink and yellow), stickers, white glue, scissors, pencil, and black marker.

Where will they hibernate? In your room, of course.

A bear mobile

1 Duplicate the templates you'll find on page 31. Draw the body twice over the brown cardboard. Also, draw the bow twice over the pink cardboard. Cut out all the pieces.

2 For arms, use the narrow tube from two small balloons, and for ears, the inflatable ends of two small balloons. For legs, use the tube from two big balloons.

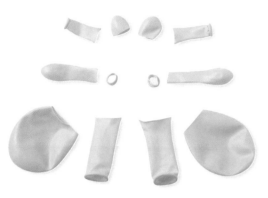

4 Decorate the bear on both sides. Make the belly and the face with stickers and put on the finishing touches with a black marker.

3 Put some glue on one side of the body. Place the ribbon, the ears, arms, and legs. Glue the other part of the body and place a ribbon to each side of the little bear. Let it dry under a heavy object.

6 Make two parallel cuts on the sides of the upper circle in the spiral and attach a ribbon on each side. Tie both ribbons. The remaining piece of ribbon is used to hang the mobile.

5 Draw a spiral inside a big circle made from green corrugated cardboard and cut it out.

7 If you want your cub to have company, make another to be its friend, but change the color of the balloons, the bows, and the stickers.

Templates

Place some tracing paper over the template you want to copy. Trace the outline with a pencil. Turn the tracing paper over and retrace the outline over the chosen bristol or cardboard.

The panda puppet, page 26

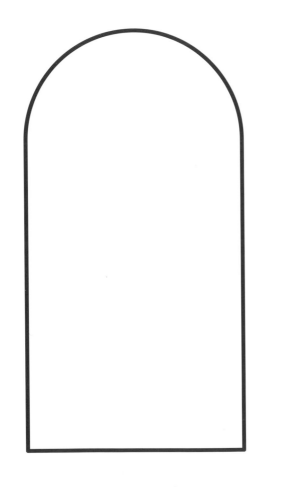

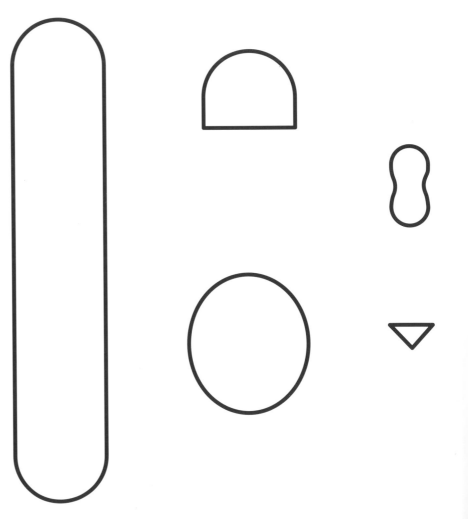

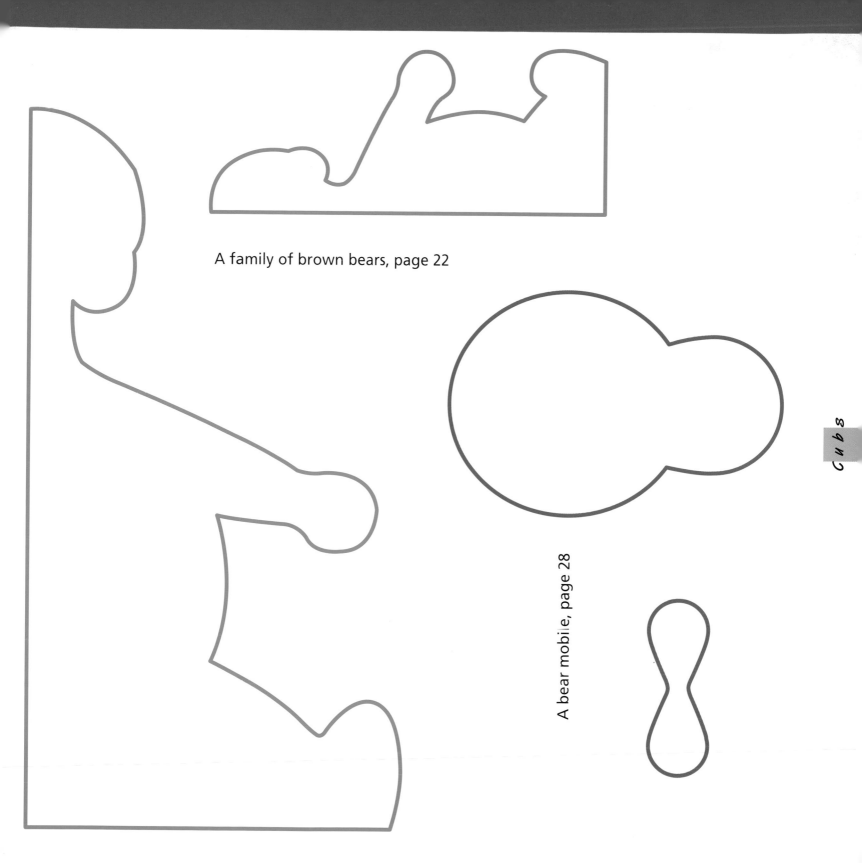

A family of brown bears, page 22

A bear mobile, page 28

We teddy bears are clever
We teddy bears are nice
Some of us can climb trees
Some can dance on ice.

We teddy bears love cuddling
We like to watch TV
We love to go to parties
and honey with our tea.

We teddy bears are special:
Whatever we can do
If we feel good, if we feel bad
It all depends on you.

So take good care of Teddy
for I belong to you
Hold me in your arms so tight
and know I love you, too.

The Teddy Bear Song